Kava Cockt& Recipes for a Relaxing Happy Hour

The Chocolate Factory

Contents

4

5

Kava Cocktails: 100 Recipes for a Relaxing Happy Hour

Kava Cocktails: 100 Recipes for a Relaxing Happy Hour is the perfect way to bring relaxation and happiness together. Whether you're looking for a fashionable new recipe or some inspiration for a classic, this cookbook will provide you with something special. With an exciting range of recipes, this book offers the perfect collection of beverages to truly make every happy hour more enjoyable.

Kava, a traditional beverage originating in the South Pacific thousands of years ago, has recently become increasingly popular as an active ingredient in modern cocktails. Select recipes appear in the book, showcasing some of the best of this emerging trend. In addition to the featured recipes, the book provides expert advice on preparing the perfect cocktail in your own unique way. Learn about the different types of spirits to use, the techniques for infusing flavors, and the essential garnishing touch to complete each beverage.

At the heart of Kava Cocktails is the desire to bring joy and relaxation into our lives, as well as providing a range of flavors to please everyone, however novice or expert. With aromas of lavender, nutmeg, lemongrass and more featured in each of the recipes' descriptions, these recipes are sure to make for a captivating happy hour. From classic twists to adventurous new combinations, each of the recipes features the refreshing taste and high spirits of Kava amongst the ingredients.

It's time to make any occasion feel special with Kava Cocktails. Perfect for a night out with friends, an intimate dinner, a romantic night, or just a quiet evening in, these recipes will bring a certain ambiance to the evening. Unwind in moments, savoring the subtle flavors and gorgeous postcsripts to end the day on. Each recipe and its instructions are designed to be straightforward and help you create your own unique experience of bliss.

Whether you're a beginner or an experienced expert, Kava Cocktails: 100 Recipes for a Relaxing Happy Hour provides the perfect companion to make nights memorable. Let's come together and create a space of relaxation and peace, and let every happy hour be an opportunity to be the best version of yourself. Here's to the journey of discovering all the possibilities and boundaries that can be achieved with Kava Cocktails!

1. Classic Kava Martini

Enjoy a taste of the south pacific with this delightfully creamy and aromatic Classic Kava Martini. The perfect way to unwind!
Serving: 2
Preparation time: 15 minutes
Ready time: 15 minutes

Ingredients:
- 2 parts Kavalactone Paste
- 4 parts chilled vodka
- Ice
- 2 teaspoons coconut cream
- 1 tablespoon simple syrup
- 2 tablespoons coconut water
- Sprig of fresh mint, for garnish

Instructions:
1. Start by combining the Kavalactone Paste and chilled vodka in a cocktail shaker.
2. Add some ice cubes and shake the mixture vigorously.
3. Then strain into a martini glass.
4. In a separate bowl, mix the coconut cream, simple syrup and coconut water until it forms a creamy mixture.
5. Pour this into the martini glass containing the Kava Martini.
6. Garnish the martini with a sprig of fresh mint.

Nutrition information:
Per Serving: Calories: 181
Total Fat: 1.2g
Saturated fat: 0.7g
Carbs: 11.5g
Protein: 0.3g
Sodium: 6mg
Fiber: 0.2g

2. Kava Colada

Kava Colada is a tropical and creamy beverage made with Kava root, rum, coconut cream, and pineapple juice. It's a balanced and refreshing drink that's perfect for summertime.
Serving: 4
Preparation time: 5 minutes
Ready time: 15 minutes

Ingredients:
• 2 ounces Kava root
• 2 ounces White Rum
• 2 ounces Coconut cream
• 2 ounces Pineapple juice

Instructions:
1. In a blender, combine Kava root, White Rum, Coconut cream, and Pineapple juice.
2. Blend for 2 minutes until smooth.
3. Serve the Kava Colada in glasses filled with ice.
4. Enjoy!

Nutrition information: Not available

3. Kava Mojito

Kava Mojito is a refreshing and tantalizing cocktail made from kava root, simple syrup, mint, white rum, and lime juice. This smooth and creamy drink is perfect for a summer day and is sure to keep you cool.
Serving: 1
Preparation Time: 5 minutes
Ready Time: 5 minutes

Ingredients:
• 1 cup fresh kava root
• 2 tablespoons of simple syrup
• 2 sprigs of fresh mint leaves
• 2 ounces white rum

- 1 lime, juiced
- Ice cubes

Instructions:

1. In a blender, combine kava root, simple syrup, and mint. Blend until smooth.
2. Add white rum and lime juice to blender and pulse until blended.
3. Place a handful of ice cubes in a glass and pour mixture over.
4. Stir and garnish with mint leaves.

Nutrition information: Per Serving, Kava Mojito contains 140 calories, 2g fat, 5g protein, and 12g carbohydrates.

4. Kava Sour

Kava Sour is a delicious and refreshing blended beverage full of flavor. This unique beverage is made with kava root, citrus juice, herbs, and spices for the perfect combination of tangy, sweet, and spicy. Whether served chilled or poured over ice, Kava Sour is a delicious alternative to traditional mixed drinks.

Serving: 2 people
Preparation time: 10 minutes
Ready time: 5 minutes

Ingredients:

- 2 tbsp. kava root powder
- Juice of 1 lime
- Juice of 1/2 lemon
- 1 tsp. lemon zest
- 1 tsp. orange zest
- 1/4 tsp. ground ginger
- 1/4 tsp. ground nutmeg
- Pinch of sea salt
- 1 tsp. honey
- 2 cups ice

Instructions:

1) In a blender, combine the kava root powder, lime juice, lemon juice, lemon zest, orange zest, ground ginger, ground nutmeg, sea salt, and honey. Blend until smooth.
2) Add the ice and blend on high until the ice is fully blended and the consistency is that of a slushy.
3) Divide between two glasses and serve.

Nutrition information:
Serving Size: 2 people
Calories: 35 kcal
Carbohydrates: 9 g
Fat: 0 g
Protein: 1 g
Sodium: 11 mg

5. Kava Punch

Kava Punch is a traditional beverage from the South Pacific Islands with a delicious blend of coconut, lime, and spices. It is an incredibly easy to make yet flavorful punch.
Serving: Serves 6
Preparation Time: 10 minutes
Ready Time: 1 hour

Ingredients:
- 3 cups canned coconut milk
- 1 cup freshly squeezed lime juice
- 2 tablespoons sliced fresh ginger
- 1 tablespoon ground vanilla bean
- 3 tablespoons sugar
- ½ teaspoon ground nutmeg

Instructions:
1. In a large pitcher, combine the coconut milk, lime juice, ginger, vanilla bean, sugar and nutmeg.
2. Stir until all of the Ingredients are well-combined.
3. Refrigerate for at least one hour to allow the flavors to blend.
4. Serve over ice.

Nutrition information: Calories: 114; Total Fat: 5.5g; Saturated Fat: 4.5g; Cholesterol: 0mg; Sodium: 20mg; Total Carbohydrate: 14.3g; Dietary Fiber: 0.9g; Sugars: 9.8g; Protein: 1.6g.

6. Kava Sunrise

Kava Sunrise is a combination of traditional Kava and fruit juice that results in a flavorful and refreshing drink.
Serving: 1
Preparation Time: 5 minutes
Ready Time: 5 minutes

Ingredients:
-2 tbsp of Kava
-1/2 cup of Mango juice
-1/2 cup of Pineapple juice
-2 tsp of Honey
-Ice cubes

Instructions:
1. In a blender, mix together the kava powder, mango juice, pineapple juice, and honey. Blend it until all the Ingredients are combined.
2. Add in the ice cubes and blend until the drink has a slushy texture.
3. Pour into a glass and enjoy!

Nutrition information:
Calories: 140, Total Fat: 0% g, Total Carbohydrate: 52% g, Protein: 4.4% g

7. Kava Margarita

Kava Margarita is a unique tropical drink that combines the flavors of a classic margarita with the deep, smooth taste of kava root. This easy-to-make beverage is sure to please your friends and family at your next gathering.
Serving: 1

Preparation time: 5 minutes
Ready time: 5 minutes

Ingredients:
- 3 ounces kava root extract
- 2 ounces lime juice
- 1 ounce simple syrup
- 2 ounces orange liqueur
- Salt, to taste

Instructions:
1. In a shaker, combine 3 ounces kava root extract, 2 ounces lime juice, 1 ounce simple syrup, and 2 ounces orange liqueur.
2. Fill a margarita glass with ice and a pinch of salt around the rim.
3. Shake the Ingredients together and strain into the glass.
4. Garnish with a lime wheel and serve.

Nutrition information:
Calories: 370 kcal, Carbohydrates: 31.1g, Protein: 0.4g, Fat: 0.07g

8. Kava Mule

Kava Mule is a tiki fruity, lime-infused take on the classic Moscow Mule made with kava root for an extra soothing kick. It has the perfect balance of sweetness and tartness which makes it very refreshing.
Serving: 1
Preparation Time: 5 minutes
Ready Time: 5 minutes

Ingredients:
• 2 ounces kava root drink
• 1-1/2 ounces lime juice
• 1-1/2 ounces simple syrup
• 2 ounces sparkling water
• ½ ounce ginger beer
• Lime wedge, for garnish

Instructions:

1. In a tall glass, combine the kava root drink, lime juice, and simple syrup.
2. Top with sparkling water.
3. Carefully pour in the ginger beer then stir everything together.
4. Serve over ice with a lime wedge garnish.

Nutrition information:
Calories: 120; Total Fat: 0g; Cholesterol: 0mg; Sodium: 0mg; Total Carbohydrates: 31g; Protein: 0g; Vitamin A: 0%; Calcium: 0%; Iron: 0%

9. Kava Spritz

Kava Spritz is a refreshing drink made from a combination of kava tea and sparkling water. It is perfect for a hot summer's day and is sure to cool you off!
Serving: Makes 2 Servings
Preparation Time: 10 Minutes
Ready Time: 10 Minutes

Ingredients:
- 2 Cups Kava tea
- 2 Cups Sparkling Water
- Lemon slices for garnishing

Instructions:
1. Heat the kava tea in a saucepan until it comes to a boil.
2. Reduce the heat and let the tea simmer for 3 more minutes.
3. Turn off the heat and let the tea cool for 4-5 minutes.
4. Divide the tea between two glasses and add 1 cup of chilled sparkling water in each glass.
5. Garnish with lemon slices and enjoy!

Nutrition information:
Calories – 320
Total Fat – 0g
Saturated fat – 0g
Cholesterol – 0mg
Sodium – 30mg

Carbohydrates – 1g
Protein – 0g

10. Kava Cosmo

Kava Cosmo is a recipe inspired by the traditional Cosmopolitan cocktail. Instead of using vodka, this version uses kava root extract as a unique and flavorful twist. With its mix of sweet and sour flavors, it's a fusion that's perfect for sipping.
Serving: 1
Preparation Time: 5 minutes
Ready Time: 5 minutes

Ingredients:
- 1/2 ounce freshly squeezed lime juice
- 1/2 ounce Kava root extract
- 1/4 ounce orange liqueur
- 1/2 ounce cranberry juice

Instructions:
1. In a shaker, combine the lime juice, kava root extract, orange liqueur, and cranberry juice.
2. Shake the Ingredients until they are well combined.
3. Strain the mixture into a martini glass.
4. Garnish with an orange slice.

Nutrition information:
Calories: 94; Fat: 0g; Sodium: 1mg; Carbohydrates: 6.6g; Sugar: 4.2g; Protein: 0g

11. Kava Paloma

Kava Paloma is a refreshing and slightly sweet tart twist on the traditional Paloma cocktail which combines the unique flavor of Kava root with citrus and honey. The perfect treat for a special occasion or just to treat yourself!
Serving: 4

Preparation Time: 10 minutes
Ready Time: 10 minutes

Ingredients:
- 2 cups of Kava root powder
- 6 ounces of fresh lime juice
- 4 ounces of light agave nectar
- 2 ounces of orange liqueur
- 1/2 teaspoon of sea salt
- 4 ounces of club soda
- 2 to 4 ounces of tequila
- Wedges of lime for garnish

Instructions:
1. In a large mixing bowl, combine Kava root powder, lime juice, agave nectar, orange liqueur and sea salt. Stir until all Ingredients are evenly incorporated.
2. Divide evenly among four glasses, fill each glass half way with the Kava mixture.
3. Top off each glass with club soda and a shot of tequila if desired.
4. Garnish with lime wedges.

Nutrition information:
Calories: 150 kcal, Carbohydrates: 16 g, Protein: 1 g, Fat: 0 g, Sodium: 320 mg

12. Kava Caipirinha

Kava Caipirinha is a perfect summer cocktail made with the popular Brazillian spirit: cachaça! It's a perfect balance of tart and sweet with the added herbaceous flavor of kava root.
Serving: 1-2
Preparation time: 5 minutes
Ready time: 5 minutes

Ingredients:
•2 ounces Cachaça
•2 teaspoons kava root powder

•2 teaspoons granulated sugar
•½ lime, cut into wedges
•Ice

Instructions:
1. Place the sugar and kava root powder in a shaker.
2. Squeeze the lime wedges into the shaker.
3. Fill the shaker with ice and cachaça.
4. Shake for about 15 seconds.
5. Strain the mixture into a tall glass filled with ice cubes.
6. Enjoy!

Nutrition information: Not available.

13. Kava Old Fashioned

Kava Old Fashioned is an aromatic twist on the classic Whiskey Old Fashioned, made from refreshing Kava root and classic cocktail Ingredients. This delicious beverage has a unique taste that features nutty and floral notes over warm spices.
Serving: Serves 1
Preparation Time: 5 minutes
Ready Time: 5 minutes

Ingredients:
• 2 ounces Kava root
• 2 dashes of aromatic bitters
• 1 teaspoon organic raw sugar
• 1 lemon wedge
• Ice cubes

Instructions:
1. Begin by filling a rocks glass with ice cubes.
2. In a separate glass, muddle the lemon wedge and raw sugar.
3. Add the muddled mixture to the rocks glass.
4. Add the kava root and bitters.
5. Stir with a spoon until all Ingredients are combined.
6. Serve and enjoy.

Nutrition information:
- Calorie: 60 kcal
- Carbs: 13 g
- Sodium: 0 mg
- Protein: 0 g
- Fat: 0 g

14. Kava Sangria

Kava Sangria is a fun and fruity take on traditional sangria, made with kava powder and fresh fruit. It's a perfect drink for a summer BBQ or get together.
Serving: 6
Preparation Time: 10 minutes
Ready Time: 15 minutes

Ingredients:
- 1/4 cup Kava Powder
- 2 cups Dry White Wine
- 1/2 cup Orange Juice
- 1/2 cup Pineapple Juice
- 1/4 cup Simple Syrup
- 1/4 cup Brandy
- 2 Tablespoons Lime Juice
- 3 cups Orange Sliced
- 2 cups Fresh Pineapple Chunks
- 1 cup Grapes

Instructions:
1. In a large pitcher, mix together the kava powder, white wine, orange juice, pineapple juice, simple syrup, brandy, and lime juice until fully incorporated.
2. Add the sliced oranges, pineapple chunks, and grapes to the pitcher and stir to combine.
3. Drop a few ice cubes into each glass and pour the sangria over the ice.
4. Garnish the glasses with a few of the fruit pieces and serve.

Nutrition information: Calories: 196 kcal, Carbohydrates: 28 g, Protein: 1 g, Fat: 0 g, Saturated Fat: 0 g, Cholesterol: 0 mg, Sodium: 5 mg, Potassium: 208 mg, Fiber: 1 g, Sugar: 24 g, Vitamin A: 77 IU, Vitamin C: 28 mg, Calcium: 20 mg, Iron: 0.6 mg

15. Kava Gimlet

Kava Gimlet is a cocktail made with Kava Kava extract, lime juice, and simple syrup, creating an exotic yet refreshing beverage.
Serving: Makes 1 drink
Preparation time: 5 minutes
Ready time: 5 minutes

Ingredients:
- 2 ounces Kava Kava extract
- 1 1/2 ounces lime juice
- 1/2 ounce simple syrup

Instructions:
1. Combine Kava Kava extract, lime juice, and simple syrup in a shaker filled with ice.
2. Shake vigorously for about 30 seconds.
3. Strain into a glass filled with ice and serve.

Nutrition information: Calories: 110, Total Fat: 0g, Sodium: 0mg, Total Carbohydrates: 14g, Protein: 0g.

16. Kava Bellini

Enjoy this delicious Kava Bellini cocktail, made with Kava Kava herb and a dry Prosecco! This refreshing libation has a natural nutty flavor and a little kick of caffeine.
Serving: 1
Preparation time: 3 minutes
Ready time: 3 minutes

Ingredients:

-1 packet of Kava Kava extract (we recommend 2 ounces per serving)
-1 bottle of Prosecco
-Ice

Instructions:
1. Add Kava Kava extract to a champagne flute.
2. Fill the glass with ice and Prosecco.
3. Stir to combine.

Nutrition information:
Calories: 161 / Fat: 0g / Protein: 0g / Carbs: 11.4 g

17. Kava Julep

Kava Julep is a traditional and delicious cocktail, made by combining vodka and coconut cream, to create a unique and refreshing drink that is perfect for any summer day.
Serving: Serves 1
Preparation time: 10 minutes
Ready time: 10 minutes

Ingredients:
-1 ½ ounces vodka
-1 ounce coconut cream
-1 teaspoon sugar
-1 teaspoon fresh lime juice
-Fresh mint or candy sprinkles to garnish

Instructions:
1. In a shaker, combine the vodka, coconut cream, sugar, and lime juice.
2. Fill the shaker with ice and shake vigorously until well-combined.
3. Strain and pour into a glass filled with crushed ice.
4. Garnish with a sprig of fresh mint or candy sprinkles.

Nutrition information: per serving: 135 calories, 4g fat, 7g sugar, 0g protein, 0g fiber.

18. Kava Negroni

Kava Negroni is a twist on the classic Italian cocktail, with an earthy flavor from an Ayurvedic infusion of Kava root.
Serving: 2
Preparation Time: 10 minutes
Ready Time: 10 minutes

Ingredients:
- 1 ounce gin
- 1 ounce Campari
- 1 ounce of Kava root infusion
- 1 ounce Aperol
- 1 wedge orange

Instructions:
1. In a tall glass, pour the gin, Campari, Kava root infusion, and Aperol over ice.
2. Stir to combine the Ingredients.
3. Cut the orange wedge and garnish the glass with it.
4. Serve chilled and enjoy.

Nutrition information:
Calories: 114
Total Fat: 0g
Cholesterol: 0mg
Sodium: 0mg
Potassium: 10.3mg
Total Carbohydrates: 8.7g
Dietary Fiber: 0.6g
Protein: 0.2g

19. Kava Piña Colada

Kava Piña Colada is a fun twist on the classic piña colada. This cocktail is made with kava root, pineapple, coconut cream, and coconut rum and is sure to be a family favorite!
Serving: Makes 1 Drink

Preparation time: 5 minutes
Ready time: 5 minutes

Ingredients:
- 2 oz Kava Root concentrate
- 1 oz coconut rum
- 2 oz pineapple juice
- 2 oz coconut cream

Instructions:
1. Place all Ingredients into a shaker or blender
2. Shake or blend until combined and creamy
3. Pour the drink into a tall glass
4. Garnish with a slice of pineapple and an umbrella

Nutrition information:
Calories: 362kcal, Carbohydrates: 25g, Protein: 2g, Fat: 4g, Sodium: 43mg, Fiber: 2g, Sugar: 19g

20. Kava Manhattan

Kava Manhattan is a delightful twist on the classic cocktail, using ground kava root to lend a unique flavor and rich texture. The result is a balanced drink that pairs well with any meal.
Serving: Serves 1
Preparation Time: 5 mins
Ready Time: 10 mins

Ingredients:
- 2 oz cognac
- 1 oz kava
- 2 dashes bitters
- 1 oz sweet vermouth
- 2 orange wedges (for garnish)

Instructions:
1. In a shaker, combine the cognac, kava, bitters, and sweet vermouth.
2. Fill a glass with ice cubes and pour the drink mixture over the cubes.

3. Squeeze the juice from one of the orange wedges into the drink and discard the wedge.
4. Garnish with the remaining orange wedge.

Nutrition information:
Calories: 200, Carbohydrates: 10 g, Proteins: 0 g, Fats: 0 g

21. Kava Fizz

Kava Fizz is a refreshing and lightly sparkling summertime drink. It's a mix of tropical coconut flavor, kava root, and citrus flavors, perfect for sipping during the summer months.
Serving: Makes 8
Preparation Time: 10 minutes
Ready Time: 10 minutes

Ingredients:
• 4 cups of coconut seltzer
• 1/2 cup passion fruit juice
• 1/2 cup pineapple juice
• 2 tablespoons kava root powder
• 2 tablespoons honey
• 1 tablespoon lime juice
• 1/4 cup chopped pineapple
• 4 slices of lime

Instructions:
1. In a large pitcher, mix together coconut seltzer, passion fruit juice, pineapple juice, kava root powder, honey, and lime juice.
2. Stir until all of the Ingredients are combined.
3. Add the chopped pineapple to the pitcher.
4. Divide the pineapple slices among 8 glasses.
5. Fill each glass with Kava Fizz and top with a pineapple slice.

Nutrition information: Per serving (8 oz): 132 Calories, 0 g fat, 0 g saturated fat, 0 mg cholesterol, 37 mg sodium, 28 g carbohydrates, 2 g fiber, 25 g sugar, and 1 g protein.

Kava Lemonade is a refreshing beverage made from Kava root and freshly-squeezed lemon juice. This beverage has a mild, earthy flavor and is said to have calming effects.
Serving: Makes 1 Serving: Preparation time: 5 minutes
Ready Time: 10 minutes

Ingredients:
- ¼ cup Kava Root Powder
- 1 ½ cups Water
- ½ cup freshly-squeezed Lemon Juice
- 1 tablespoon Honey
- Ice Cubes

Instructions:
1. Place the Kava Root Powder in a bowl and pour over the Water.
2. Stir vigorously until the Kava Root powder has dissolved.
3. Strain the mixture into a glass, removing any pieces of root.
4. Add Lemon Juice and Honey and mix until fully combined.
5. Add Ice Cubes to the glass and stir together.

Nutrition information:
Calories: 91, Fat: 0 g, Sodium: 10 mg, Carbohydrates: 24 g, Protein: 1 g

The Kava Daiquiri is an exotic twist on the classic Daiquiri cocktail, combining the flavors of pineapple, lime, and the traditional Polynesian root Kava. This rum-based drink is sure to tantalize your taste buds.
Serving: 1
Preparation time: 5 minutes
Ready time: 10 minutes

Ingredients:
• 2 ounces silver rum
• ½ lime, juiced

- ½ pineapple, peeled and roughly chopped
- 2 tablespoons kava powder
- 1 teaspoon simple syrup

Instructions:
1. In a blender, combine the rum, lime juice, pineapple, kava powder, and simple syrup.
2. Blend the mixture until smooth.
3. Pour the kava daiquiri into a glass.
4. Serve and enjoy!

Nutrition information:
Calories- 203, Total fat- 0.2g, Sodium- 3.8mg, Potassium-144mg, Total carb- 12.5g, Protein- 0.9g

24. Kava Screwdriver

Kava Screwdriver is a delightful mocktail that is perfect for any special occasion. It is both fun to look at and delicious to taste.
Serving: 4
Preparation time: 10 minutes
Ready time: 10 minutes

Ingredients:
-1 cup pineapple juice
-¼ cup kava concentrate
-Ice, to serve
-2 tablespoons orange juice

Instructions:
1. In a small jug, mix together the pineapple juice and kava concentrate.
2. Stir until the kava concentrate is completely mixed with the juice.
3. Add some ice to each glass and pour the kava screwdriver over the ice.
4. Top with orange juice and stir.

Nutrition information:
Calories: 68, Carbohydrates: 21g, Protein: 1g, Fat: 0g, Cholesterol: 0mg, Sodium: 7mg, Potassium: 102mg, Sugar: 16g

Kava Collins is a delicious take on the classic Tom Collins cocktail. Featuring a fruity twist, this cocktail is sure to be a hit at any party.
Serving: Makes 1 drink
Preparation Time: 3 minutes
Ready Time: 3 minutes

Ingredients:
- 2 ounces kava concentrate
- ½ ounce fresh lemon juice
- ½ ounce simple syrup
- 2 ounces club soda
- Lemon twist for garnish

Instructions:
1. In a mixing glass, combine kava concentrate, lemon juice, and simple syrup.
2. Fill a collins glass with ice cubes.
3. Pour the mixture over the ice cubes.
4. Top with club soda.
5. Stir to combine.
6. Garnish with a lemon twist.

Nutrition information: Not available.

26. Kava Sour Apple Martini

Kava Sour Apple Martini is a deliciously sweet and tart drink perfect for a girls night out or special occasion. With the combination of Kava root extract, apple juice, and lemon juice, this martini will be sure to have everyone coming back for more!
Serving: Serves 1
Preparation Time: 5 minutes
Ready Time: 5 minutes

Ingredients:
- 2 ounces Kava root extract
- 2 ounces apple juice or cider
- 1 ounce lemon juice
- ½ ounce simple syrup or honey
- Ice

Instructions:
1. Fill a shaker with ice and add the Kava root extract, apple juice, lemon juice, and simple syrup.
2. Shake vigorously for about 30 seconds, then strain the mixture into a martini glass.
3. Garnish with a slice of apple or lemon wedge and enjoy!

Nutrition information:
Calories: 128 kcal, Carbohydrates: 17.1 g, Protein: 0.6 g, Fat: 0.1 g, Saturated Fat: 0 g, Sodium: 8 mg, Potassium: 98 mg, Fiber: 0.3 g, Sugar: 13.9 g, Vitamin A: 44 IU, Vitamin C: 7.7 mg, Calcium: 11 mg, Iron: 0.3 mg

27. Kava Bee's Knees

Kava Bee's Knees is a delicious cocktail combining kava powder, honey simple syrup, and gin that is wonderfully smooth and herbal.
Serving: Makes 2 cocktails
Preparation Time: 10 minutes
Ready Time: 10 minutes

Ingredients:
- 1 teaspoon kava root powder
- 2 ounces gin
- 1 ounce freshly squeezed lemon juice
- 1 ounce honey simple syrup

Instructions:
1. In a small bowl, mix together the kava powder with one ounce of hot water and stir until all lumps are gone.

2. In a cocktail shaker, add the kava mixture, gin, lemon juice, and honey simple syrup and fill with ice.
3. Shake vigorously for about 10 seconds.
4. Strain into two rocks glasses filled with fresh ice.
5. Garnish with lemon wedges and serve.

Nutrition information: Calories: 241, Carbohydrates:16.8g, Protein: 0.4g, Fat: 0.1g, Sodium 2.8mg

28. Kava White Russian

Kava White Russian is an interesting twist on the classic drink. The combination of kava and flavored vodka adds a hint of botanical flavor and creates a relaxing, unique experience. The chilled cream and classic vodka also help to create a smooth and creamy texture.
Serving: 1
Preparation time: 5 minutes
Ready time: 5 minutes

Ingredients:
• 2 ounces Kava Koffee Vodka
• 1 tablespoon of your favorite flavored syrup
• 1 ounce cold cream
• Ice

Instructions:
1. Fill a highball glass with ice
2. Pour the Kava Koffee Vodka, syrup and cold cream over the ice
3. Stir to mix and chill the drink
4. Enjoy!

Nutrition information: Per serving (1 drink): Calories: 270, Fat: 13g, Saturated Fat: 8g, Cholesterol: 40mg, Sodium: 15mg, Carbohydrates: 20g, Sugar: 15g, Protein: 2g.

29. Kava Palmetto

Kava Palmetto is a delicious Caribbean dish, a stew of plantains and starchy root vegetables cooked in a savory coconut curry sauce. It is an easy dish to make and great for feeding a crowd.

Serving: Makes 5 servings.
Prep Time: 10 minutes
Ready Time: 30 minutes

Ingredients:
-2 tbsp vegetable oil
-1 onion, chopped
-3 cloves garlic, minced
-1 tsp fresh ginger, grated
-2 large plantains, sliced into rounds
-1 sweet potato, diced
-1 yam, diced
-1 red bell pepper, diced
-2 cups vegetable broth
-1 can coconut milk
-1 tbsp curry powder
-Salt and pepper

Instructions:
1. In a large pot, heat oil over medium-high heat.
2. Add onion and sauté for 5 minutes or until soft.
3. Add garlic and ginger and sauté for 1 minute.
4. Add plantains, sweet potato, yam, and bell pepper and stir to combine.
5. Add vegetable broth, coconut milk, curry powder, salt, and pepper.
6. Reduce heat to low, cover, and simmer for 20 minutes or until vegetables are cooked through.
7. Serve Kava Palmetto with cooked rice or your favorite grain, and enjoy!

Nutrition information: Per serving (1/5th of recipe): 414 calories, 24 g fat, 33 g carbohydrates, 21 g sugar, 3 g protein

30. Kava Caipiroska

Kava Caipiroska is an alcoholic drink made with vodka, kava, and lime. It's a great way to relax and unwind after a long day.
Serving: Makes 1 drink
Preparation time: 10 minutes
Ready time: 10 minutes

Ingredients:
- 3 ounces vodka
- 3 Tablespoons kava concentrate
- Juice from 1 lime
- 2 tablespoons raw honey
- 1 cup crushed ice

Instructions:
1. In a blender, combine the vodka, kava concentrate, lime juice and honey.
2. Blend over medium speed for about 1 minute, or until smooth.
3. Add in the crushed ice and blend again, making sure everything is combined
4. Pour into a martini glass and serve immediately.

Nutrition information:
Calories: 200, Total Fat: 0g, Saturated Fat: 0g, Trans Fat: 0g, Cholesterol: 0mg, Sodium: 0mg, Carbohydrates: 16g, Fiber: 0g, Sugar: 14g, Protein: 0g.

31. Kava Mojito Mocktail

Kava Mojito Mocktail is a refreshing and delicious drink that is perfect for hot summer days. This fruity mocktail is made with natural Ingredients such as kava, mint, lime juice, and coconut water so you can enjoy a light and delicious beverage anytime you like.
Serving: serves 2
Preparation time: 5 minutes
Ready time: 10 minutes

Ingredients:
-2 teaspoons kava paste

-handful of fresh mint leaves
-¼ cup lime juice
-1 cup coconut water
-1 teaspoon honey (optional)
-Ice cubes

Instructions:
1. In a glass, muddle together the fresh mint leaves and kava paste until they are well combined.
2. Add the lime juice to the mix and stir.
3. Add the coconut water to the mix and stir until everything is well blended.
4. If desired, add the honey and stir until it is mixed in.
5. Fill the glass with ice cubes and mix everything together.
6. Garnish with a sprig of mint and serve.

Nutrition information
Calories: 38, Carbohydrates: 8g, Protein: 1g, Sodium: 79.6mg, Sugar: 4g

32. Kava Pineapple Express

A tropical twist to a traditional favorite, Kava Pineapple Express is a sweet and savory pineapple-flavored cocktail made with Waka Kava and pineapple juice.
Serving: Makes one cocktail
Preparation time: 5 minutes
Ready time: 5 minutes

Ingredients:
√ 2 oz Waka Kava (instant kava concentrate)
√ 4 oz pineapple juice
√ Ice cubes
√ Lime wedge (for garnish)

Instructions:
1. Fill a glass or shaker with 3-4 ice cubes.
2. Measure Waka Kava and pineapple juice into the glass.
3. Stir well until combined.

4. Garnish with a lime wedge.

Nutrition information: Calories 167, Fat 0g, Sodium 5mg, Carbohydrates 11g, Sugar 10g, Protein 0g.

33. Kava Coconut Margarita

Kava Coconut Margarita is a special tropical twist on the classic cocktail. With the addition of kava and creamy coconut milk, this drink is sure to be a hit with your guests!
Serving: Makes 1 drink
Preparation time: 5 minutes
Ready time: 5 minutes

Ingredients:
• 2 ounces kava root extract
• 2 ounces coconut milk
• 1 ounce freshly squeezed lime juice
• 2 ounces white tequila
• ½ ounce simple syrup
• Lime slices, for garnish

Instructions:
1. In a shaker, combine kava, coconut milk, lime juice, tequila, and simple syrup.
2. Shake until well blended, about 1 minute.
3. Strain the margarita into an ice-filled glass.
4. Garnish with lime slices.

Nutrition information: Calories 280, Total Fat 2.5 g, Cholesterol 0 mg, Sodium 4 mg, Total Carbohydrate 19 g, Dietary Fiber 0 g, Sugars 17 g, Protein 0 g.

34. Kava Watermelon Smash

Kava Watermelon Smash is an invigorating summer drink which combines the ancient ceremonial beverage - kava - with watermelon - the classic summer treat. It's a delicious way to celebrate the heat of the season.

Serving: 1
Preparation time: 15 mins
Ready time: 15 mins

Ingredients:
- Coolsome Kava Drink Packet
- 250ml sparkling water
- 1 cup watermelon cubes

Instructions:
1. In a blender, combine the watermelon cubes with the Coolsome Kava Drink Packet.
2. Pour the mixture into a glass and add the sparkling water.
3. Stir the mixture gently with a spoon.

Nutrition information: Per serving - 37 calories, 2.5 g Fat, 3.8 g carbohydrates, 2 g protein.

35. Kava Bloody Mary

Kava Bloody Mary is the perfect combination of the classic, refreshing Bloody Mary blended with earthy Kava Kava for a unique twist. It's a perfect brunch beverage with a stress-free twist.

Serving: 1 beverage
Preparation time: 5 minutes
Ready time: 5 minutes

Ingredients:
- 2 shots (or 2oz) vodka
- 2tsp Kava Kava Root Powder
- 4 oz tomato juice
- ¼ tsp Worcestershire sauce
- 1 tsp lime juice
- Hot sauce and celery salt to taste

Instructions:

1. In a cocktail shaker, combine vodka, Kava Kava Root Powder, tomato juice, Worcestershire sauce, and lime juice.
2. Add a few dash of hot sauce and celery salt to taste.
3. Fill the shaker with ice and shake for 10-15 seconds.
4. Strain into a glass with ice.
5. Garnish with a celery stalk and a lime wedge.

Nutrition information: Calories: 105, Total Fat: 0g, Sodium: ≥472mg, Total Carbohydrate: 4g, Sugars: 3g, Protein: 0g

36. Kava Tropical Punch

Kava Tropical Punch is an exotic and flavorful non-alcoholic beverage bursting with tropical fruits. Its creamy texture and sweet flavor is sure to tantalize your taste buds and make you feel like you're in an island paradise!
Serving: 4
Preparation Time: 10 minutes
Ready Time: 15 minutes

Ingredients:
• 1/2 cup kava paste
• 2 cups crushed ice
• 1 can (15.5 oz) unsweetened pineapple chunks
• 1 cup orange juice
• 1/2 cup frozen mango chunks
• 2 tablespoons honey or agave syrup
• 2 tablespoons lime juice
• 1 cup coconut milk

Instructions:
1. In a blender, combine kava paste, crushed ice, pineapple chunks, orange juice, mango chunks, honey, lime juice, and coconut milk.
2. Blend until creamy and smooth.
3. Serve in glasses garnished with tropical fruit slices.

Nutrition information:
• Calories: 157

- Fat: 7.6g
- Carbs: 22.7g
- Protein: 3.4g

37. Kava Pineapple Mojito

The Kava Pineapple Mojito is a unique and flavorful mix of tropical pineapple and coconut flavors with a hint of kava for a summery and slightly tropical twist. It's a fun and refreshing beverage perfect for warm summer days!
Serving: 2-3
Preparation Time: 10 minutes
Ready Time: 10 minutes

Ingredients:
- 2 ounces of white Rum
- 2 ounces of Coconut Water
- 2 ounces of Pineapple Juice
- 1 ounce of Kava Extract
- 1-2 tablespoons of Honey
- 2 tablespoons of Lime Juice
- Handful of Mint Leaves
- Ice Cubes

Instructions:
1. In a blender, combine the white rum, coconut water, pineapple juice, kava extract, honey, and lime juice.
2. Blend until all the Ingredients are mixed together.
3. Place a few ice cubes in a glass and pour the blended mixture over the cubes.
4. Add the mint leaves and a few more ice cubes to the glass.
5. Stir the mixture and enjoy the Kava Pineapple Mojito.

Nutrition information:
Calories: 125 kcal
Carbohydrates: 16 g
Protein: 1 g
Fat: 0 g

Saturated Fat: 0 g
Unsaturated Fat: 0 g
Cholesterol: 0 mg
Sodium: 13 mg
Potassium: 236 mg
Fiber: 1 g
Sugar: 11 g
Vitamin A: 10 IU
Vitamin C: 7.6 mg
Calcium: 13 mg
Iron: 0.2 mg

38. Kava Grapefruit Martini

This Kava Grapefruit Martini is a unique and refreshing way to kick off your next dinner party or gathering. Combining the tropical tang of fresh grapefruit juice with Kava's earthy taste and just a hint of sweet, this cocktail is sure to be a hit no matter your guests!
Serving: Serves 2
Preparation Time: 10 minutes
Ready Time: 10 minutes

Ingredients:
- 1/2 cup Kava root
- 1/3 cup freshly squeezed grapefruit juice
- 2 tablespoons of orange juice
- 2 tablespoons of sugar
- 2 tablespoons of vodka
- Ice

Instructions:
1. Place Kava root and 1/4 cup of hot water in a blender and pulse for 1 minute until Kava is fully dissolved.
2. Strain the Kava mixture into two martini glasses.
3. In a shaker, combine the grapefruit juice, orange juice, sugar, and vodka.
4. Fill the shaker with ice and shake for 1 minute.
5. Pour the mixture into the martini glasses.

Nutrition information:
Calories: 182, Fat: 0g, Cholesterol: 0mg, Sodium: 8mg, Carbohydrates: 13g, Protein: 0.5g

39. Kava Basil Smash

Kava Basil Smash is a healthy, flavorful drink that is perfect any time of year. It is sweet, refreshing, and has a hint of herbal flavor from basil and honey. It's a great way to get your daily dose of vitamin C and other vitamins and minerals.
Serving: 1-2
Preparation time: 10 minutes
Ready time: 10 minutes

Ingredients:
• 2 lemons, cut into wedges
• 2 tablespoons of honey
• 2 tablespoons of fresh basil, chopped
• 2 teaspoons of dried kava powder
• 2 cups of cold water

Instructions:
1. In a medium bowl, combine the lemon wedges, honey, basil, and kava powder.
2. Using a muddler or wooden spoon, press down on the Ingredients to release the flavors and aromas.
3. Add the cold water, stirring to combine.
4. Strain the drink using a fine mesh sieve into two glasses, and enjoy!

Nutrition information
Per serving: 40 calories, 0g fat, 9g carbohydrates, 0g protein.

40. Kava Cucumber Cooler

Refresh with this zesty Kava Cucumber Cooler, perfect for a hot summer day!

Serving: 5
Preparation Time: 10 minutes
Ready Time: 1 hour

Ingredients:
- 2 pounds cucumbers, peeled and chopped
- 2 cups kava root powder
- 1 lemon, sliced
- 4 cups cold water
- 1/4 cup honey
- Mint leaves, chopped (optional)

Instructions:
1. In a large container, combine the cucumber, kava root powder, lemon slices, and cold water.
2. Stir the mixture until the kava root powder is completely dissolved.
3. Add honey and stir until well combined.
4. Refrigerate the Kava Cucumber Cooler for 1 hour before serving.
5. Serve the Kava Cucumber Cooler over ice, garnished with the mint leaves if desired.

Nutrition information:
- Calories: 170 kcal
- Protein: 1 g
- Total Fat: 0 g
- Total Carbohydrates: 40 g
- Sodium: 30 mg
- Fiber: 3 g

41. Kava Elderflower Spritz

Enjoy this light and refreshing cocktail – Kava Elderflower Spritz – perfect for hosting or just to enjoy at home with friends and family alike. This simple recipe requires only a few Ingredients and is sure to please!
Serving: 8
Preparation time: 10 minutes
Ready time: 25 minutes

Ingredients:
- 2 1/2 cups of fresh kava root
- 15 ml elderflower cordial
- 2 cups of dry white wine
- 8 wedges of lime
- 2 tablespoons of simple syrup
- 1 bottle of sparkling water
- Ice cubes

Instructions:
1. Start by crushing the kava root in a mortar and pestle until it becomes a fine powder.
2. In a large pitcher, mix together the kava powder, elderflower cordial, white wine, lime wedges, and simple syrup.
3. Stir until combined and allow to sit for 15 minutes.
4. After 15 minutes, add the sparkling water and stir until fully incorporated.
5. Place the ice cubes in each glass, then pour the mixture into the glasses and serve.

Nutrition information:
Calories: 58, Total Fat: 0 g, Saturated Fat: 0 g, Cholesterol: 0 mg, Sodium: 1 mg, Carbohydrates: 5 g, Dietary Fiber: 0 g, Sugar: 5 g, Protein: 0 g

42. Kava Blueberry Lemonade

Cool off on a hot summer day with Kava Blueberry Lemonade. This fruity and refreshing beverage is a perfect treat for those this looking for a low calorie pick-me-up.
Serving: 4
Preparation Time: 5 minutes
Ready Time: 10 minutes

Ingredients:
- 2.5 cups of fresh blueberries
- 2.5 cups of freshly squeezed lemon juice
- 2 tsp of kava root powder

- 3 cups of cold water
- 2 tablespoons of honey

Instructions:

1. In a blender, combine 1 cup of blueberries, 1 cup of lemon juice and 1 teaspoon of kava root powder. Blend until a smooth consistency is achieved.
2. Pour the mixture into a large pitcher, and add the remaining blueberries, lemon juice, kava powder and honey. Stir until combined.
3. Add in the cold water and stir.
4. Serve over ice and enjoy!

Nutrition information:

Calories: 77 Calories; Total Fat: 0g; Saturated Fat: 0g; Cholesterol: 0mg; Sodium: 2mg; Total Carbohydrates: 19g; Dietary Fiber: 2g; Sugars: 15g; Protein: 1g

43. Kava Mango Tango

Kava Mango Tango is a refreshing tropical smoothie with kick from Kava root - the sweet summer taste of mango and kava root comes together in this energizing smoothie.Serving: 2 Preparation time: 10 minutes Ready time: 10 minutes

Ingredients:
-1/2 cup mango puree
-1/2 cup Kava root powder
-1 banana
-1 cup almond milk
-1 teaspoon honey
-1 teaspoon vanilla extract

Instructions:

1. In a blender, combine the mango puree, Kava root powder, banana, almond milk, honey and vanilla extract.
2. Blend until smooth and creamy.
3. Serve immediately.

Nutrition information:
Calories: 150; Total Fat: 4g; Saturated Fat: 1g; Trans Fat: 0g; Cholesterol: 0mg; Sodium: 16mg; Carbohydrates: 24g; Dietary Fiber: 4g; Sugars: 16g; Protein: 5g; Vitamin A: 1%; Calcium: 10%; Iron: 2%

44. Kava Passion Fruit Margarita

This Kava Passion Fruit Margarita is a refreshing summer cocktail that combines the natural sedative properties of Kava with the sweet-tart flavor of passion fruit. Enjoy the unique relaxing flavor of this twist on a classic Margarita!
Serving: 4
Preparation Time: 5 minutes
Ready Time: 5 minutes

Ingredients:
• ½ cup of ice
• 2 ounces of Kava
• 2 ounces of passion fruit puree
• 2 ounces of orange-flavored liqueur
• 1 ounce of lime juice
• Lime slices and sugar for garnish

Instructions:
1. Fill up a shaker with the ice, Kava, passion fruit puree, orange-flavored liqueur, and lime juice and shake vigorously.
2. Strain into 4 glasses and garnish with lime slices and sugar.
3. Enjoy this refreshing Kava Passion Fruit Margarita!

Nutrition information: Per Serving: 170 calories, 0 g fat, 3.5 g protein, 22g carbohydrates, 0mg cholesterol, 10mg sodium.

45. Kava Raspberry Fizz

Kava Raspberry Fizz is a refreshing beverage that combines kava tea and raspberry syrup to make a unique summer drink.
Serving: 4

Preparation Time: 10 minutes
Ready Time: 40 minutes

Ingredients:

2 teaspoons kava powder, 2 cups hot water, 2 tablespoons raspberry syrup, 2 tablespoons mint, handful of ice cubes.

Instructions:

1. Mix 1 teaspoon of kava powder into the hot water and let steep for 5 minutes.
2. Place the raspberry syrup, mint, and the remaining teaspoon of kava powder in separate serving glasses.
3. Strain the kava tea and divide it equally between the glasses.
4. Add 2-3 ice cubes to each glass.
5. Serve and enjoy!

Nutrition information (per serving): Calories: 20, Total Carbohydrates: 5g, Protein: 0g, Fat: 0g, Sodium: 0g.

46. Kava Ginger Lemonade

Kava Ginger Lemonade is a summertime treat that combines the earthy and herbal flavor of kava root with the refreshing taste of ginger and lemon. This drink is sure to provide a unique and invigorating experience.
Serving: Serves 1
Preparation Time: 5 minutes
Ready Time: 5 minutes

Ingredients:
• 2 tsp of Kava root powder
• ¼ cup freshly squeezed lemon juice
• 2 tsp dark brown sugar
• 2 dashes of ground ginger
• 1 cup of water
• 2-3 Ice cubes

Instructions:

1. In a small bowl, mix together the Kava root powder, dark brown sugar, and ground ginger.
2. Add the freshly squeezed lemon juice and water and stir until all the Ingredients are combined evenly.
3. Pour the mixture into a tall glass, add the ice cubes and stir until cool.

Nutrition information:
Calories: 16 kcal, Carbohydrates: 4g, Fat: 0g, Protein: 0g, Cholesterol: 0mg, Sodium: 2.4mg, Potassium: 31mg, Sugar: 4g, Vitamin C: 10.6mg.

47. Kava Spiced Cider

This warming, spiced cider is the perfect remedy for a chilly winter's day. Created with a hint of kava root powder, this drinks offers a cozy feeling of relaxation. Serve up with a cinnamon stick for an extra delicious accent.
Serving: 4
Preparation Time: 5 minutes
Ready Time: 10 minutes

Ingredients:
• 8 cups apple cider
• 1 teaspoon of kava root powder
• 8 cinnamon sticks
• 2 teaspoon of ground nutmeg
• Honey or maple syrup to taste

Instructions:
1. Place the cider in a large pot.
2. Add in the kava root powder and stir until it is completely dissolved.
3. Place the cinnamon sticks in the pot and stir.
4. Add the nutmeg and stir.
5. Place the pot over high heat and bring to a boil.
6. Reduce the heat to low and simmer for 10 minutes.
7. Add honey or maple syrup to taste.
8. Ladle the cider into mugs and serve with a cinnamon stick.

Nutrition information: Calories: 142, Total Fat: 1 g, Sodium: 169 mg, Total Carbohydrates 34 g, Fiber: 4 g, Sugars: 29 g, Protein: 2 g.

48. Kava Peach Bellini

This Kava Peach Bellini is a classic summer cocktail with just 4 Ingredients and a few simple steps. It's sweet, bubbly, and full of peach flavor - perfect for a relaxing summer evening!
Serving: Serving: 4
Preparation time: Preparation Time: 5 minutes
Ready time: Ready Time: 5 minutes

Ingredients:
- 1 bottle Prosecco
- 1 cup sparkling peach nectar
- 1/4 cup freshly squeezed orange juice
- 2 shots KAVA Peach Bellini Liqueur

Instructions:
1. Pour Prosecco, sparkling peach nectar, orange juice and KAVA Peach Bellini Liqueur into a pitcher and stir to combine.
2. Divide mixture among four glasses and enjoy.

Nutrition information per serving: Calories 200, Total Fat 0g, Cholesterol 0mg, Sodium 0mg, Total Carbohydrates 20g, Protein 0g, Vitamin A 0%, Vitamin C 20%, Calcium 0%, Iron 0%.

49. Kava Lavender Lemonade

Kava Lavender Lemonade is a refreshing, relaxing blend of kava, lavender, and lemonade. Perfect for a relaxing afternoon or evening drink.
Serving: 4
Preparation Time: 10 minutes
Ready Time: 10 minutes

Ingredients:

- 2 cups of kava tea
- 2 lemons, juiced
- 2 cups of water
- 2 tablespoons of lavender extract
- 2 tablespoons of honey
- Ice

Instructions:
1. Prepare kava tea by following instructions on the kava package.
2. Juice the lemons and set aside the juice.
3. Combine the kava tea, lemon juice, water, lavender extract, and honey in a large pitcher and stir together.
4. Fill each glass halfway with ice and top off with the kava lavender lemonade mixture.
5. Garnish each glass with a lemon wedge and enjoy!

Nutrition information:
Calories: 105
Total Fat: 0g
Saturated Fat: 0g
Cholesterol: 0mg
Sodium: 2mg
Carbohydrates: 27g
Fiber: 0g
Sugar: 22g
Protein: 0g

50. Kava Strawberry Daiquiri

Kava strawberry daiquiri is a delicious and refreshing cocktail that is packed with flavor. This twist on a classic daiquiri combines creamy kava with sweet strawberries to create the perfect summer drink.
Serving: 2
Preparation time: 10 minutes
Ready time: 10 minutes

Ingredients:
- 2 ounces kava

- 2 ounces strawberry puree
- 2 ounces fresh lime juice
- 2 ounces simple syrup
- 2 dashes Angostura bitters
- 2 ounces light rum
- Ice, for Serving:

Instructions:

1. In a cocktail shaker, combine the kava, strawberry puree, lime juice, simple syrup and Angostura bitters.
2. Fill the shaker halfway with ice and shake vigorously for 30 seconds.
3. Strain into two glasses filled with ice.
4. Top each glass with 1 ounce of rum and stir gently to combine.
5. Garnish with a strawberry slice and a lime wheel and serve.

Nutrition information:calories per serving: 220, total fat: 0g, saturated fat: 0g, cholesterol: 0mg, sodium: 4mg, total carbohydrates: 19g, dietary fiber: 0g, protein: 0g.

51. Kava Hibiscus Cooler

This is an easy and refreshing Kava Hibiscus Cooler that you can make any time of the year. Enjoy this light and flavorful beverage that is perfect for a hot summer day.
Serving: 1
Preparation Time: 5 minutes
Ready Time: 5 minutes

Ingredients:
- ½ cup Kava Kava root
- 2 tablespoons honey
- 1 tablespoons dried hibiscus flowers
- 2 cups cold water
- Ice

Instructions:
1. Grind Kava Kava root as finely as possible.

2. In a small saucepan, add honey and hibiscus flowers and bring to a boil.
3. Once boiled, reduce heat to low and add the ground Kava Kava root, stirring constantly and ensuring it does not burn.
4. After about 4 minutes, remove from heat and strain.
5. In a large cup, add the strained Kava and Hibiscus mixture to cold water and stir.
6. Add ice to the cup and enjoy!

Nutrition information:
Calories: 50, Fat: 0g, Carbohydrates: 11g, Protein: 0g, Fiber: 0g, Sugar: 11g

52. Kava Orange Creamsicle

Kava Orange Creamsicle is a unique and tasty take on the classic combination of orange creamsicle, but with a special twist - kava! This recipe will bring an island-inspired flavor to your kitchen for a creamy and refreshing treat.
Serving: 4-6
Preparation Time: 10 minutes
Ready Time: 5-10 minutes

Ingredients:
- 1/2 cup Kava Kava Root Powder
- 3 cups almond milk
- 1/2 teaspoon vanilla extract
- 2 tablespoons real orange zest
- 1/4 cup raw honey
- 1/4 cup freshly squeezed orange juice (from 1-2 oranges)
- 1/2 teaspoon orange extract

Instructions:
1. In a blender, add Kava Kava Root Powder, almond milk, vanilla extract, orange zest, raw honey, orange juice, and orange extract.
2. Blend until everything is smooth.
3. Pour the mixture into popsicle molds.
4. Freeze for 5-10 minutes, or until desired firmness.

5. Enjoy!

Nutrition information:
Per Serving: 130 Cal, 1.6g Fat, 23.4g Carbs, 0.2g Protein

53. Kava Pineapple Punch

Kava Pineapple Punch is an incredible tropical flavored drink that is sure to become a favorite. It is full of flavor and easy to prepare.
Serving: 8
Preparation time: 5 minutes
Ready time: 10 minutes

Ingredients:
-1 cup of fresh Pineapple, diced
-1 cup of Coconut Milk
-1/4 cup of Kava Powder
-1 teaspoon of Pure Vanilla Extract
-4 teaspoons of Brown Sugar
-1 cup of Cold Water

Instructions:
1. In a blender, combine diced pineapple, coconut milk, kava powder, vanilla extract and brown sugar.
2. Blend the Ingredients together until they are fully mixed and creamy.
3. Pour the Ingredients into a pitcher with cold water.
4. Stir the Kava Pineapple Punch and serve chilled.

Nutrition information: Per 8oz of Kava Pineapple Punch contains 58 calories, 1.0g fat, 11.3g carbohydrates, 0.7g protein, 0.4g dietary fiber, and 28 mg sodium.

54. Kava Raspberry Mojito

Kava Raspberry Mojito is a refreshing twist on a classic summer favorite. Sweet raspberries and fragrant mint leaves are muddled with beer kava to

create a unique and delicious drink perfect for backyard barbecues or patio parties.
Serving: Makes 2
Preparation time: 10 minutes
Ready time: 10 minutes

Ingredients:
-1½ cups frozen raspberries
-4 mint leaves, plus more for garnish
-1 teaspoon sugar
-½ cup kava beer
-1 ounce lime juice
-4 tablespoons pineapple juice
-Ice

Instructions:
1. In a large glass, muddle together raspberries, mint leaves, and sugar.
2. Add kava beer, lime juice, and pineapple juice. Stir to combine.
3. Fill glasses with ice and pour in mojito mix.
4. Garnish with additional mint leaves if desired.

Nutrition information: Per serving: 140 calories; 2.5 g fat; 30 g carbohydrates; 2.5 g protein; 4 mg sodium; 1 g fiber.

55. Kava Mint Julep

Kava Mint Julep is a tropical spin on the classic julep recipe, made with kava root powder, mint leaves, and simple syrup.
Serving: Makes 1 drink
Preparation time: 5 minutes
Ready time: 5 minutes

Ingredients:
-1 teaspoon kava root powder
-4 fresh mint leaves
-2 teaspoons simple syrup
-Crushed ice
-1/2 cup cold water

Instructions:

1. Place the kava root powder, mint leaves, and simple syrup in a shaker or jar.
2. Gently muddle the Ingredients together with a spoon or muddler.
3. Fill the shaker with crushed ice and water.
4. Secure the lid and shake vigorously for 1 minute.
5. Strain the mixture into a glass filled with crushed ice.
6. Garnish with extra mint leaves and enjoy!

Nutrition information: Per serving: Calories 120, Total Fat 0g (0% DV), Sodium 7mg (0% DV), Total Carbohydrate 32g (12% DV), Sugars 27g, Protein 0g.

56. Kava Grapefruit Spritz

This fresh and tangy Kava Grapefruit Spritz is a perfect drink for any occasion. It's a tantalizing combination of the light, floral kava and sharp, tart grapefruit that refreshes and revives your taste buds.

Serving: 4
Preparation Time: 10 minutes
Ready Time: 10 minutes

Ingredients:
• 1 cup of freshly squeezed grapefruit juice
• 2 tablespoons of sugar
• 2 cups of brewed kava tea
• 2 cups of sparkling water
• 2 tablespoons of fresh orange juice
• Ice cubes

Instructions:

1. In a large pitcher, combine the freshly squeezed grapefruit juice, sugar, brewed kava tea, sparkling water, and fresh orange juice. Stir until the sugar has dissolved.
2. Fill 4 glasses with ice cubes. Divide the kava grapefruit spritz mixture among the glasses.

3. Garnish with fresh or dried grapefruit slices, and orange slices if desired.

Nutrition information:
Calories: 73kcal, Carbohydrates: 15.5g, Protein: 0.7g, Fat: 0.1g, Saturated Fat: 0g, Sodium: 7.3mg, Potassium: 153.5mg, Fiber: 0.7g, Sugar: 14.3g, Vitamin C: 32.3mg, Calcium: 4.7mg, Iron: 0.2mg

57. Kava Blackberry Smash

Kava Blackberry Smash is a delicious and refreshing drink that is perfect for hot summer days. It's a great way to cool down while enjoying the flavor of fresh summer blackberries.
Serving: 4
Preparation Time: 10 minutes
Ready Time: 20 minutes

Ingredients:
- 2 cups of frozen blackberries
- 2 tablespoons of fresh-squeezed lemon juice
- 1 tablespoon of kava powder
- 2 tablespoons of honey
- 4 cups of cold water
- Ice cubes

Instructions:
1. In a blender, combine the frozen blackberries, lemon juice, kava powder, honey, and cold water.
2. Blend the mixture until it is well combined and smooth.
3. Pour the mixture into glasses over ice cubes.
4. Garnish with fresh blackberries.

Nutrition information:
Serving Size: 1 cup
Calories: 60
Total Fat: 0g
Sodium: 5mg
Total Carbohydrates: 16g

Sugars: 11.5g
Protein: 0g

58. Kava Apple Cider Punch

Enjoy an autumn twist on a classic with this Kava Apple Cider Punch! An easy-to-make, refreshing, and cozy beverage, this punch will be sure to get your gatherings started in no time.
Serving: 4
Preparation time: 10 minutes
Ready time: 10 minutes

Ingredients:
- 2 cups fresh apple cider
- 4 tablespoons kava concentrate
- 2 tablespoons fresh lemon juice
- 2 tablespoons honey or agave
- ½ teaspoon ground cinnamon
- Pinch of ground nutmeg
- Ice cubes

Instructions:
1. In an empty pitcher, add the apple cider, kava concentrate, lemon juice, honey, cinnamon, and nutmeg.
2. Stir well to combine.
3. Add the ice cubes and stir gently.
4. Serve in glasses and enjoy!

Nutrition information (Per Serving):
Calories: 140 kcal, Carbohydrates: 31 g, Protein: 0.3 g, Fat: 0.2 g, Saturated Fat: 0.1 g, Sodium: 1 mg, Fiber: 0.6 g, Sugar: 28 g

59. Kava Caramel Appletini

Enjoy this delicious twist on a classic cocktail with this Kava Caramel Appletini! Sweet, creamy and filled with flavors of caramel and fresh apple, you won't regret trying this recipe.

Serving: 2
Preparation Time: 5 minutes
Ready Time: 5 minutes

Ingredients:
- 2 shots of Kava
- 2 shots of Caramel Vodka
- 2 shots of Apple Schnapps
- 5 ounces of freshly squeezed apple juice
- Apple slice for garnish

Instructions:
1. In a mixing glass, combine the kava, caramel vodka, apple schnapps, and freshly squeezed apple juice.
2. Stir until the Ingredients are completely incorporated.
3. Put a few ice cubes into two martini glasses.
4. Strain the mixture into the martini glasses.
5. Garnish with an apple slice and enjoy!

Nutrition information:
- Calories: 210
- Total Fat: 0g
- Cholesterol: 0mg
- Sodium: 2mg
- Total Carbohydrates: 16g
- Protein: 0g

60. Kava Mango Margarita

Kava Mango Margarita is an exotic and interesting combination of the classic mango flavor with the relaxing effects of Kava root. This twist on a classic margarita is sure to surprise and delight your taste buds!
Serving: Makes 1 cocktail
Preparation time: 5 minutes
Ready time: 5 minutes

Ingredients:
- 3 ounces mango juice

- 1/2 ounce lime juice
- 1/4 ounces Kava Kava concentrate
- 1 teaspoon agave nectar
- 1/2 ounce triple sec

Instructions:
1. In a shaker filled with ice, combine the mango juice, lime juice, Kava Kava concentrate, agave nectar, and triple sec.
2. Shake vigorously until all Ingredients are incorporated.
3. Strain the mixture into a martini or margarita glass.
4. Garnish with a lime wheel and enjoy!

Nutrition information: Not available

61. Kava Berry Bliss

Kava Berry Bliss is a sweet and tart fruit medley that is sure to satisfy any dessert craving!
Serving: 4
Preparation time: 10 minutes
Ready time: 1 hour

Ingredients:
• 2 cups fresh strawberries, sliced
• 1 cup blueberries
• 1 cup raspberries
• 2 tablespoons honey
• 1 teaspoon ground kava root

Instructions:
1. Preheat oven to 350°F (175°C).
2. In a large bowl, combine the strawberries, blueberries, and raspberries.
3. Drizzle the honey over the top and mix until the fruit is evenly coated.
4. Spread the mixture in an 8x8-inch baking dish.
5. Sprinkle the kava root over the fruit.
6. Bake for 45-50 minutes, until the fruit is bubbly and lightly browned.
7. Allow the Kava Berry Bliss to cool before serving.

Nutrition information:
Serving size: 1/4 of recipe
Calories: 96
Fat: 0.6g
Saturated fat: 0.1g
Unsaturated fat: 0.4g
Carbohydrates: 24g
Fiber: 4.2g
Sugar: 17g
Protein: 1.8g

62. Kava Spicy Mule

This delicious Kava Spicy Mule is a great way to give a twist to the renowned Moscow Mule. The Kava variant is made with herbaceous Kava and a spicy ginger beer, resulting in an unrivalled flavor.
Serving: 1
Preparation time: 5 minutes
Ready time: 5 minutes

Ingredients:
- 180ml (3/4 cup) ginger beer
- 45ml (3 tablespoons) Kava
- 15ml (1 tablespoon) lime juice
- 5ml (1 teaspoon) ginger syrup

Instructions:
1. Pour ginger beer, Kava, lime juice, and ginger syrup into a copper mug.
2. Stir all Ingredients together.
3. Garnish with a lime wedge and enjoy!

Nutrition information (per serving):
Calories: 110, Total Fat: 0g, Cholesterol: 0mg, Sodium: 30mg, Total Carbohydrate: 25g, Sugars: 22g, Protein: 0g

Kava Pineapple Ginger Mocktail is a perfect drink for a warm day that packs a punch without the added alcohol. It is a cold, refreshing concoction that is full of flavors.

Serving: 4
Preparation Time: 5 minutes
Ready Time: 5 minutes

Ingredients:
- 2 cups pineapple juice
- 2 cups coconut water
- 1/4 cup fresh or canned pineapple chunks
- 2 tablespoons fresh lime juice
- 2 tablespoons fresh ginger, chopped
- 2 tablespoons kava root powder

Instructions:
1. In a medium-sized bowl, combine the pineapple juice, coconut water, pineapple chunks, lime juice, and ginger.
2. Mix well and refrigerate for at least 1 hour before serving.
3. When ready to serve, add the kava root powder and mix well.
4. Pour the mocktail into individual glasses and enjoy.

Nutrition information: Per Serving: 130 calories; 0.4g fat; 9.9g carbohydrates; 1.2g protein

Kava Lemon Lavender Collins is a unique, combination of flavors that come together to create a one-of-a-kind drink. Made with kava, lemon, lavender, and syrup, this cocktail brings out sophisticated and refreshing notes.

Serving: Serves 1
Preparation Time: 5 minutes
Ready Time: 5 minutes

Ingredients:

- 2 parts kava
- 1 part fresh lemon juice
- 1/2 part lavender syrup
- 2 parts soda water

Instructions:
1. In a glass, mix together kava, fresh lemon juice and lavender syrup.
2. Add soda water and stir until all Ingredients are mixed together.
3. Garnish with a slice of lemon or lavender sprig and serve.

Nutrition information: Calories: 75, Total Fat: 0g, Saturated Fat: 0g, Cholesterol: 0mg, Sodium: 94mg, Carbohydrates: 19g, Fiber: 0g, Sugar: 7g, Protein: 0g.

65. Kava Raspberry Bellini

Kava Raspberry Bellini is a fruity twist on a classic summer cocktail. Enjoy this combination of light sparkling wine, kava, and raspberry puree for a smooth and refreshing warm-weather treat.
Serving: 4
Preparation time: 5 minutes
Ready time: 5 minutes

Ingredients:
• 1 bottle of demi-sec sparkling wine, chilled
• 2 tablespoons of kava powder
• ½ cup of raspberry puree
• 1 tablespoon of lemon juice

Instructions:
1. Combine the raspberry puree and kava powder in a bowl and whisk until smooth.
2. Pour the sparkling wine into a pitcher and add the raspberry kava mixture.
3. Stir the mixture and add the lemon juice.
4. Divide the bellini among 4 glasses and serve.

Nutrition information: (per serving)

Calories: 116
Fat: 0 g
Carbohydrates: 8 g
Protein: 0.5 g

66. Kava Cherry Limeade

Kava Cherry Limeade is a delicious and refreshing summery drink that is perfect for any time of year! A combination of kava and cherry-limeade syrup gives it a unique flavor that is sure to be a hit.
Serving: 4-6
Preparation time: 10 minutes
Ready time: 10 minutes

Ingredients:
- 1/2 cup Kava root powder
- 2 cups Cherry-Limeade syrup
- 2 litres filtered Carbonated water

Instructions:
1. In a large pitcher, combine the Kava root powder, Cherry-Limeade syrup and filtered Carbonated water.
2. Stir until the Ingredients are fully combined.
3. Refrigerate for at least 1 hour.
4. Serve over ice.

Nutrition information (per serving):
Calories: 140
Fat: 0g
Carbohydrates: 36g
Protein: 0g
Sodium: 250mg

67. Kava Strawberry Basil Lemonade

Escape the summer heat with the refreshing flavor of Kava Strawberry Basil Lemonade! This delicious beverage is sure to keep you cool all summer long.
Serving: 10
Preparation Time: 10 minutes
Ready Time: 1 hour

Ingredients:
• 4 cups fresh or prepared lemonade
• 4 pitted medjool dates
• 2 tablespoons freshly grated ginger
• 1 tablespoon kava root powder
• 1 pound strawberries, chopped
• 2 tablespoons fresh basil, chopped
• 2 tablespoons lime juice

Instructions:
1. In a blender, blend together the lemonade, dates, ginger, kava root powder, and lime juice until completely smooth.
2. Pour the blended mixture into a large pitcher.
3. Add the chopped strawberries and basil.
4. Stir until evenly combined.
5. Let the mixture sit for 1 hour for the flavors to combine.
6. Serve over ice with a sprig of basil.

Nutrition information: Calories: 150, Fat: 0g, Cholesterol: 0mg, Sodium: 20mg, Carbohydrates: 38g, Fiber: 3g, Sugar: 34g, Protein: 1g

68. Kava Citrus Spritz

Kava Citrus Spritz is a tropical-inspired summer cocktail bursting with a combination of fresh citrus flavors and kava tea. This recipe is an easy way to cool down in the summertime while also enjoying a subtly sweet, guilt-free treat.
Serving: 1
Preparation Time: 5 minutes
Ready Time: 5 minutes

Ingredients:
- 2 ounces kava tea
- Juice of 1 lime
- Juice of 1 lemon
- 1-2 tablespoon cane sugar, depending on how sweet you want the drink to be
- 2 ounces sparkling water
- 1 wedge of lime, for garnish

Instructions:
1. In a shaker, add kava tea, lime juice, lemon juice and cane sugar.
2. Shake vigorously for about 30 seconds.
3. Add sparkling water and stir to combine.
4. Pour over ice and garnish with a wedge of lime.

Nutrition information:
Calories: 92
Total Fat: 0 g
Saturated Fat: 0 g
Cholesterol: 0 mg
Sodium: 10 mg
Carbohydrates: 24 g
Fiber: 0 g
Sugar: 22 g
Protein: 0 g

69. Kava Peach Mojito

Kava Peach Mojito is a delicious and refreshing summer drink. With the sweet flavor of peaches, the zesty taste of mint and the natural nutty flavor of Kava, this cocktail is sure to hit the spot!
Serving: 4
Preparation time: 10 minutes
Ready time: 15 minutes

Ingredients:
- 2 peaches

- 1/4 cup of Kava root
- 2 tablespoons of lime juice
- 4 tablespoons of sugar
- 1 bunch of fresh mint leaves
- 2 cups of sparkling water
- Ice

Instructions:
1. Peel and cut the peaches into small pieces.
2. In a blender, combine Kava root, lime juice, and sugar. Blend until smooth.
3. Add the peach pieces, sparkling water, and fresh mint leaves to the blender. Blend until desired consistency.
4. Pour the mixture into glasses filled with ice and serve.

Nutrition information: per serving (4):
Calories: 200
Fat: 0g
Carbs: 46g
Protein: 2g
Sugar: 32g

70. Kava Blueberry Martini

This delicious Kava Blueberry Martini combines Ingredients such as fresh blueberries, fresh mint, vodka, and Kava concentrate for an unforgettable sweet and fruity taste.
Serving: Makes 1 martini
Preparation time: 5 minutes
Ready time: 5 minutes

Ingredients:
- 1 cup fresh blueberries
- 1 sprig mint
- 2 ounces vodka
- 1 ounce Kava concentrate
- Ice

Instructions:
1. In a shaker, muddle the blueberries and mint.
2. Add the vodka and Kava concentrate. Shake for 30 seconds.
3. Add the ice and shake for an additional 30 seconds.
4. Strain the mixture into a martini glass.

Nutrition information:
Calories: 250, Total Fat: 0g, Sodium: 6mg, Potassium: 152mg, Total Carbohydrates: 12g, Protein: 1g

71. Kava Ginger Beer Float

Kava Ginger Beer Float is a delicious and refreshing summertime treat that combines the flavors of ginger beer and sweet cream for a bubbly and crowd-pleasing snack.
Serving: 4
Preparation Time: 5 minutes
Ready Time: 10 minutes

Ingredients:
- 2 bottles of ginger beer
- 3 tablespoons kava kava root powder
- 4 scoops of ice cream
- 1/4 teaspoon ground cardamom
- 1/4 teaspoon ground ginger
- ¼ cup whipped cream

Instructions:
1. In a saucepan, heat ginger beer until it starts to bubble.
2. Add kava powder, cardamom, and ginger, stirring to combine.
3. Reduce heat to low and simmer for 5 minutes, stirring occasionally.
4. Remove from heat and let cool for 10 minutes.
5. Place one scoop of ice cream in each of four glasses.
6. Pour equal amounts of the kava mixture into the glasses.
7. Top with whipped cream and serve.

Nutrition information:
Serving Size: 1

Calories: 210
Total Fat: 15g
Saturated Fat: 12g
Cholesterol: 75mg
Sodium:120mg
Total Carbohydrates: 16g
Sugars: 11g
Protein: 4g

72. Kava Watermelon Mojito

Kava Watermelon Mojito is a delicious, refreshing summer time beverage that is a perfect way to cool down! It is made with natural kava root, ripe watermelon, mint, and lime, creating a flavorful and unique mixture of flavors.
Serving: 2
Preparation Time: 5 minutes
Ready Time: 5 minutes

Ingredients:
- 1/2 cup ripe watermelon, cubed
- 4 tablespoons kava liquid concentrate
- 2 tablespoons fresh lime juice
- 2 tablespoons simple syrup
- 6-8 mint leaves
- 1 cup of ice

Instructions:
1. In a blender, add the watermelon, kava liquid concentrate, lime juice, simple syrup, and mint leaves.
2. Blend until smooth.
3. Pour the mixture into a glass and add the ice.
4. Stir to combine and enjoy!

Nutrition information:
Calories: 135
Total Fat: 0g
Cholesterol: 0mg

Sodium: 11mg
Total Carbohydrate: 32.2g
Sugar: 19.5g
Protein: 1.7g

73. Kava Blackberry Lemonade

Refreshing and sweet, Kava Blackberry Lemonade is a delicious and easy drink to make. Perfect for the warm summer days, this delicious drink will quench your thirst and satisfy your sweet tooth.
Serving: 4 people
Preparation Time: 5 minutes
Ready Time: 30 minutes

Ingredients:
- 2 ounces Kava Root Liquid Extract
- 1 cup frozen blackberries
- 1/2 cup honey or maple syrup
- 4 lemons, juiced
- 2 cups cold water
- Crushed ice

Instructions:
1. In a blender, combine the Kava Root Liquid Extract, frozen blackberries, honey or maple syrup, and the freshly juiced lemons. Pulse until well blended.
2. Pour the mixture into a large pitcher, add cold water, and stir until evenly combined.
3. Fill a glass with crushed ice and pour the Kava Blackberry Lemonade over the ice.
4. Serve cold and enjoy.

Nutrition information:
Per serving:
Calories: 220, Fat: 0g, Saturated Fat: 0g, Trans Fat: 0g, Carbohydrates: 49g, Sugar: 40g, Protein: 2.5g, Sodium: 3mg, Fiber: 6.5g.

74. Kava Coconut Lime Spritz

Kava Coconut Lime Spritz is a refreshing and invigorating drink that combines the calming properties of kava, the sweetness of coconut, and the tartness of lime for an uplifting and delicious treat.
Serving: 6-8
Preparation time: 10 minutes
Ready time: 10 minutes

Ingredients:
• 2 cups kava root
• 1 cup coconut milk
• Juice of 1 lime
• 2 tablespoons honey
• 1 cup cold sparkling water
• Optional: 2 sprigs of fresh mint, for garnish

Instructions:
1. In a blender, combine the kava root, coconut milk, lime juice, honey, and cold sparkling water. Blend on high until all of the Ingredients are fully combined.
2. Pour the spritz into desired glasses and garnish with fresh mint, if desired.
3. Serve immediately. Enjoy!

Nutrition information: Per serving, Kava Coconut Lime Spritz provides approximately 122 calories, 4g of protein, 8g of carbohydrates, 2g of fat, and 0mg of cholesterol.

75. Kava Raspberry Mint Smash

A refreshing beverage made of Kava root, raspberry, mint, and coconut water, Kava Raspberry Mint Smash is a simple yet exotic way to get your caffeine fix.
Serving: Makes 1 Serving: Preparation Time: 10 minutes
Ready Time: 10 minutes

Ingredients:

- 2 tablespoons Kava root
- 1 tablespoon freshly diced mint leaves
- ½ cup fresh raspberries
- 2 shares coconut water
- Ice

Instructions:
1. Put Kava root and mint in a blender.
2. Add raspberries and blend until mixture is smooth.
3. Pour in coconut water and blend again.
4. Pour the mixture into a glass filled with ice and enjoy!

Nutrition information (per serving):
Calories: 80, Total Fat: 0g, Saturated Fat: 0g, Cholesterol: 0mg, Sodium: 0mg, Total Carbohydrates: 17g, Dietary Fiber: 4g, Sugar: 11g, Protein: 1g

76. Kava Mango Pineapple Punch

Kava Mango Pineapple Punch is a perfect way to quench your thirst with a refreshing and unique combination of flavors. Its sweet and tart components combine to make a delicious and rejuvenating summer treat.
Serving: 6-8
Preparation Time: 15 mins
Ready Time: 15 mins

Ingredients:
• 2 large mangoes, peeled and cut into small pieces
• 1 cup fresh pineapple chunks
• 2 tablespoons honey
• 1/2 teaspoon instant kava powder
• 2 cups cold water
• Ice cubes

Instructions:
1. In a blender, combine the mangoes, pineapple chunks, honey, kava powder, and water.
2. Blend until mixture is smooth.
3. Pour punch into glasses filled with ice cubes and serve.

Nutrition information:
- Calories: 68 kcal
- Total Fat: 0 g
- Saturated Fat: 0 g
- Trans Fat: 0 g
- Cholesterol: 0 mg
- Sodium: 10 mg
- Total Carbohydrates: 17 g
- Dietary Fiber: 1 g
- Sugar: 13 g
- Protein: 0.6 g

77. Kava Blood Orange Margarita

Kava Blood Orange Margaritas offer an invigorating and refreshing twist on a classic cocktail. This updated concoction features the bold flavor of kava, mixed with tart and sweet blood orange juice.
Serving: Makes 1
Preparation Time: 5 minutes
Ready Time: 5 minutes

Ingredients:
- 1.5 ounces of kava
- 1 ounce of triple sec
- 2 ounces of fresh blood orange juice
- 2 ounces of fresh lime juice
- Ice
- 1/2 teaspoon of agave

Instructions:
1. In a cocktail shaker, combine the kava, triple sec, blood orange juice, lime juice, and agave.
2. Fill the shaker with ice and shake for approximately 30 seconds or until all of the Ingredients are mixed together well.
3. Strain the mixture into a chilled stem glass.
4. Garnish the margarita with a slice of lime and enjoy!

Nutrition information:
Calories: 153, Carbohydrates: 12.7g, Protein: 0.4g, Fat: 0.2g, Cholesterol: 0mg, Sodium: 4mg, Potassium: 65mg, Sugar: 9.9g.

78. Kava Honeydew Cooler

Enjoy a cool and refreshing Kava Honeydew Cooler. This is a fusion of organic Mediterranean honey, sweet honeydew melon, and Floridian Kava – a plant-based superfood that gives this drink a mildly nutty flavor.
Serving: Makes two 8 floz servings
Preparation time: 5 minutes
Ready time: 5 minutes

Ingredients:
- 2 cups cubed honeydew melon
- 8fl oz Floridian Kava
- 1/4 tsp organic mediterranean honey
- Ice cubes

Instructions:
1. Place the honeydew melon cubes into a blender and blend on high speed until thoroughly combined.
2. Once blended, add in the Floridan Kava and blend for an additional 30 seconds.
3. Pour the mixture into two 8 floz glasses filled with ice cubes.
4. Gently stir in ¼ teaspoon of organic Mediterranean honey into each glass.
5. Serve cold and enjoy!

Nutrition information:
Serving Size: 8 floz
Calories: 50 kcal
Fat: 0 g
Carbohydrates: 12 g
Protein: 0.5 g

79. Kava Strawberry Kiwi Mojito

Take the traditional Mojito cocktail and add a tropical, fruity twist with this delicious Kava Strawberry Kiwi Mojito. With fresh strawberries, kiwi, and just the right amount of rum, this drink is sure to be an interesting and tasty addition to any gathering.
Serving: One serving.
Preparation time: 5 minutes.
Ready time: 7 minutes.

Ingredients:
-1.5 ounces of white rum
-2 sprigs of mint
-2 tablespoons of simple syrup
-4 ounces of kiwi puree
-4 ounces of strawberry puree
-1 lime wedge
-Seltzer water

Instructions:
1. Fill an old-fashioned glass with all of the Ingredients except the seltzer water.
2. Muddle the Ingredients.
3. Fill the glass with ice and top off with the seltzer water.
4. Garnish with a lime wedge.

Nutrition information
Calories: 123
Fat: 0g
Carbohydrates: 14g
Protein: 0g

80. Kava Rosemary Grapefruit Fizz

Kava Rosemary Grapefruit Fizz is a sparkling drink made from kava tea, fresh grapefruit, and sprigs of rosemary. Perfect to kick off a special occasion, this drink is sure to quench any thirst.
Serving: 4

Preparation Time: 5 minutes
Ready Time: 5 minutes

Ingredients:
-4 cups cold kava tea
-1/4 cup freshly squeezed grapefruit juice
-2 tablespoons white sugar
-1 tablespoon rosemary leaves
-2 cups chilled seltzer

Instructions:
1. In a large pitcher, mix together kava tea, grapefruit juice, sugar, and rosemary. Stir until sugar is completely dissolved.
2. Add seltzer and mix until all Ingredients are combined.
3. Serve in glasses over ice and enjoy!

Nutrition information:
Calories: 100, Sodium: 35mg, Total carbohydrate: 21g, Sugars: 17g, Protein: 1g

81. Kava Coconut Raspberry Lemonade

Enhance your summer experience with this zesty Kava Coconut Raspberry Lemonade that is a great way to relax and cool off.
Serving: 2
Preparation Time: 5 minutes
Ready Time: 10 minutes

Ingredients:
- 2 tablespoons of Kava concentrate
- 2 tablespoons of raw honey
- 2 cups of coconut water
- 1/2 cup of raw organic raspberry juice
- 2 tablespoons of freshly squeezed lemon juice

Instructions:
1. In a shaker add Kava concentrate, raw honey, coconut water, raspberry juice and lemon juice.

2. Give the mixture a few shakes until everything is well-combined.
3. Strain the mixture into glass with a few ice cubes added.
4. Serve and enjoy!

Nutrition information:
Calories: Aprox. 97 kcal,
Fat: 0 g,
Carbs: 24 g,
Protein: 1 g.

82. Kava Pineapple Coconut Mojito

Kava Pineapple Coconut Mojito is a vibrant and refreshing beverage that tastes like a tropical vacation in a glass! This drink is easy to prepare and can be enjoyed any time of year.
Serving: 4
Preparation time: 15 minutes
Ready time: 15 minutes

Ingredients:
- 4 ounces of Kava
- 2 ounces lime juice
- 1/2 cup of pineapple juice
- 2 tablespoons of coconut cream
- 6 ounces of club soda
- 6 sprigs of mint
- Pineapple wedges and mint leaves for garnish

Instructions:
1. In a large pitcher or container, mix together 4 ounces of Kava, 2 ounces of lime juice, 1/2 cup of pineapple juice, and 2 tablespoons of coconut cream.
2. Stir until all the Ingredients are combined and the liquid is even in consistency.
3. Fill four glasses with ice and divide the homemade kava mixture into the glasses.
4. Top off each glass with one and a half ounces of club soda and stir until combined.

5. Garnish each glass with two sprigs of mint, a pineapple wedge, and a mint leaf.

Nutrition information: Each serving of Kava Pineapple Coconut Mojito contains 89 calories, 0.1g of fat, 21.4g of carbohydrates, 0.1g of protein, and 0.3g of dietary fiber.

83. Kava Mango Basil Margarita

Enjoy a tropical twist on your favorite classic cocktail with this Kava Mango Basil Margarita. This flavor-packed concoction features fresh mango, basil, and kava for a delightful tropical taste.
Serving: 2
Preparation Time: 5 minutes
Ready Time: 10 minutes

Ingredients:
• 2 ounces kava infused tequila
• 2 ounces mango puree
• 1 ounce lime juice
• 2-3 fresh basil leaves
• 2 tablespoons agave nectar
• Ice cubes

Instructions:
1. In a cocktail shaker, add tequila, mango puree, lime juice, basil leaves, and agave nectar.
2. Shake the mixture to combine.
3. Add the ice cubes to two glasses.
4. Strain the margarita mixture into the glasses and garnish with a slice of fresh mango and basil leaves.

Nutrition information: Per serving (two drinks): about 350 calories, 0 g fat, 0 mg cholesterol, 29 g carbohydrates, 1 g protein, 10 mg sodium, 2 g fiber.

Kava Blueberry Lavender Lemonade is a refreshing summer treat perfect for a hot day. This tart and sweet drink can be enjoyed cold or hot.
Serving: 6
Preparation Time: 15 minutes
Ready Time: 15 minutes

Ingredients:
- 1 cup of kava
- 2 cups of lavender flowers
- 4 cups of fresh or frozen blueberries
- 1-2 lemons Juiced
- 1/2 cup of sugar
- 2 cups of water

Instructions:
1. Place kava, lavender, blueberries, lemon juice and sugar into a large pot over medium-high heat.
2. Bring to a boil and reduce heat to low.
3. Simmer for 10 minutes, stirring occasionally.
4. Take off heat and add 2 cups of water to the mixture.
5. Let cool for 5 minutes.
6. Strain into a glass pitcher.
7. Serve cold or hot.

Nutrition information:
- Calories: 100
- Fat: 0g
- Cholesterol: 0mg
- Sodium: 5mg
- Carbohydrates: 25g
- Fiber: 2g
- Protein: 2g

85. Kava Cucumber Mint Spritz

Enjoy this classic summer spritz, featuring the cooling flavors of cucumber and mint and a hint of tartness from the Kava.
Serving: 4
Preparation Time: 5 minutes
Ready Time: 5 minutes

Ingredients:
- 1 cucumber (peeled and thinly sliced)
- 4 ounces Kava
- 2 tablespoons fresh mint leaves (plus extra for garnish)
- 2 tablespoons freshly squeezed lime juice
- 8 ounces club soda

Instructions:
1. Divide the cucumber slices among 4 glasses.
2. In a blender, combine Kava, mint leaves and lime juice. Blend until well combined.
3. Add the Kava mixture to the glasses and top with club soda.
4. Garnish with more mint leaves and enjoy.

Nutrition information (Per Serving):
- Calories: 52
- Total fat: 0g
- Cholesterol: 0mg
- Sodium 47mg
- Total Carbohydrates: 3g
- Dietary Fiber: 1g
- Protein: 0g

86. Kava Spicy Paloma

Kava Spicy Paloma is a tequila-based Mexican drink that emphasizes the flavors of grapefruit and jalapenos for an enjoyable and unique blend of sweet and spicy. This cocktail is zesty and is sure to be a hit at parties or barbecues!
Serving: This recipe makes one portion of Kava Spicy Paloma.
Preparation time: 5 minutes.
Ready time: 5 minutes.

Ingredients:
- 2 ounces tequila
- 2 ounces freshly squeezed pink or red grapefruit juice
- 1/4 teaspoon finely chopped jalapeno (optional)
- 1/2 teaspoon lime juice
- 1 teaspoon agave nectar
- 6 ounces club soda

Instructions:
1. In a tall glass, mix together the tequila, grapefruit juice, jalapeno, lime juice and agave nectar.
2. Fill the glass with ice and stir together.
3. Top with club soda and stir together once more.
4. Garnish with a lime wedge or jalapeno slice if desired.

Nutrition information
Serving: 1 drink
Calories: 133 kcal
Carbohydrates: 16.2g
Protein: 0.2g
Fat: 0g
Saturated Fat: 0g
Cholesterol: 0mg
Sodium: 13.9mg
Potassium: 42.6mg
Fiber: 0g
Sugar: 11.1g
Iron: 0.2mg

87. Kava Cranberry Ginger Punch

Try this delicious and refreshing Kava Cranberry Ginger Punch. It is perfect for any occasion!
Serving: Makes 4
Preparation Time: 5 minutes
Ready Time: 5 minutes

Ingredients:
- 2 ½ cups cranberry juice
- 2 tablespoons kava powder
- 2 tablespoons freshly grated ginger
- ¼ cup lime juice
- 1 cup soda water
- Lime wedges (optional, for garnish)

Instructions:
1. In a large pitcher, mix together cranberry juice, kava powder, ginger, and lime juice.
2. Add the soda water and stir to combine.
3. Pour over ice into four glasses.
4. Garnish with lime wedges, if desired.

Nutrition information: Serving size: 1, Calories: 105, Total Fat: 0g, Cholesterol: 0mg, Sodium: 5mg, Total Carbohydrate: 25g, Protein: 2g, Vitamin A: 2%, Vitamin C: 25%.

88. Kava Raspberry Peach Bellini

Enjoy the cool and refreshing taste of this raspberry peach bellini mixed with Kava, which adds a unique flavor to the classic drink.
Serving: 6
Preparation Time: 10 minutes
Ready Time: 10 minutes

Ingredients:
- 2 ½ cups fresh or frozen raspberries
- 2 ½ cups fresh or frozen peaches
- 2 cups white grape juice
- 1 cup Kava
- ½ cup sugar

Instructions:
1. In a blender, combine raspberries, peaches and white grape juice. Blend until smooth.

2. Pour mixture into a large bowl and stir in Kava and sugar until sugar is completely dissolved.
3. Pour raspberry peach Kava mixture into a pitcher and chill before serving.

Nutrition information: Per serving (6): Total calories 211, Carbohydrates 52 g, Protein 1 g, Fat 0 g, Sodium 5 mg.

89. Kava Watermelon Basil Mojito

This refreshing Kava Watermelon Basil Mojito combines the tropical flavors of Kava, Watermelon, and Basil with the sweetness of Coconut and Mint, creating a delicious and unique cocktail experience.
Serving: 2-4
Preparation Time: 10 minutes
Ready Time: 25 minutes

Ingredients:
- 1/4 cup of Kava Kava
- 1/2 cup of Coconut Water
- 1 cup of diced Watermelon
- 2 tablespoons of freshly squeezed Lime Juice
- 2 tablespoons of fresh Basil, chopped
- 6-8 Mint Leaves, plus extra for garnish
- 2 tablespoons of Coconut Sugar
- 2 tablespoons of White Rum

Instructions:
1. Combine the kava, coconut water, watermelon, lime juice, basil, mint, and coconut sugar in a blender and blend on high speed until combined.
2. In a large pitcher, combine the blended mixture with the white rum and stir to combine.
3. Give it a taste and adjust sweetness to your preference.
4. Fill 2-4 glasses with crushed ice and pour the mojito into each glass.
5. Garnish each glass with a couple of mint leaves.

Nutrition information (Per Serving): Calories: 150 kcal; Carbohydrates: 15 g; Protein: 1 g; Fat: 0.5 g; Saturated Fat: 0 g;

Cholesterol: 0 mg; Sodium: 33 mg; Potassium: 124 mg; Fiber: 1 g; Sugar: 7 g; Vitamin A: 68 IU; Vitamin C: 14 mg; Calcium: 29 mg; Iron: 1 mg.

90. Kava Strawberry Kiwi Spritzer

Kava Strawberry Kiwi Spritzer is the perfect refreshing summer drink made with naturally sweet strawberries and kiwi. Each sip of this bubbly spritzer will give you an invigorating burst of energy!
Serving: 4-6
Preparation Time: 10 minutes
Ready Time: 10 minutes

Ingredients:
• 2 cups of fresh strawberries diced
• 2 kiwis diced
• 2 tablespoons of kava powder
• 2 tablespoons of lime juice
• 4 cups of cold club soda

Instructions:
1. In a large bowl combine the diced strawberries and kiwi.
2. Add the kava powder and lime juice and mix together until the kava powder is evenly distributed.
3. Pour the mix into a large pitcher and fill with cold club soda.
4. Stir the mixture together and serve with ice.

Nutrition information:
Calories: 68 kcal
Fat: 0 g
Carbohydrates: 17 g
Protein: 1 g

91. Kava Pineapple Mango Smash

Kava Pineapple Mango Smash is an island-inspired cocktail, combining juicy mango and pineapple juices with creamy coconut milk and earthy Kava. Perfect for summer celebrations or poolside lounging!
Serving: 4
Preparation time: 10 minutes
Ready time: 10 minutes

Ingredients:
- 4 ounces of Kava
- 4 ounces of freshly squeezed mango juice
- 4 ounces of freshly squeezed pineapple juice
- 4 ounces of coconut milk
- 2 tablespoons of sugar or honey (optional)

Instructions:
1. In a cocktail shaker combine Kava, mango juice, pineapple juice, and coconut milk.
2. Shake vigorously until fully combined.
3. If desired, add sugar or honey for sweetness.
4. Pour into four glasses.
5. Garnish with a pineapple slice or mango cube.

Nutrition information: For the Kava Pineapple Mango Smash, the calories per serving are approximately 177 calories per serving. It contains 8.2g of fat, 24.9g of carbohydrates, and 1.3g of protein.

92. Kava Rosemary Grapefruit Spritz

Enjoy the best of summer's bounty with this Kava Rosemary Grapefruit Spritz, featuring grapefruit and rosemary-infused vodka. The slightly tart and herbaceous flavors are balanced with a hint of sweetness from St. Germain elderflower liqueur and kava tea.
Serving: 1
Preparation time: 15 minutes
Ready time: 15 minutes

Ingredients:
2 ounces grapefruit and rosemary-infused vodka

½ ounce St. Germain elderflower liqueur
1 tablespoon kava tea
2 ounces fresh pink grapefruit juice
2 dashes orange bitters
1 sprig of rosemary for garnish

Instructions:
1. In a shaker fill with ice.
2. Pour in vodka, liqueur, kava tea, grapefruit juice, and orange bitters.
3. Shake vigorously for 30 seconds until chilled.
4. Strain into a Collins or rocks glass with fresh ice.
5. Garnish with a sprig of rosemary.

Nutrition information: Not available.

93. Kava Coconut Lime Mojito

This Kava Coconut Lime Mojito packs an island punch of flavors. With the tart lime, sweet coconut and unique notes of kava, it'll take you away from the everyday.
Serving: One drink
Preparation time: 5 minutes
Ready time: 5 minutes

Ingredients:
- 3 ounces kava root beverage
- 3 ounces limeade
- 1 tablespoon lime juice
- 2 tablespoons shaved coconut
- 1/4 cup freshly sliced lime
- Ice
- Mint
- Soda water

Instructions:
1. In a cocktail shaker, combine 2 ounces of kava root beverage, 2 ounces of limeade, 1 tablespoon of lime juice, 2 tablespoons of shaved coconut, and 1/4 cup of freshly sliced lime.

2. Add ice, shake until well combined.
3. Strain the drink into a tall glass filled with ice.
4. Fill the glass with soda water.
5. Garnish with mint and extra lime slices.

Nutrition information:
Calories: 80, Total Fat: 0g, Saturated Fat: 0g, Trans Fat: 0g, Cholesterol: 0mg, Sodium: 5mg, Total Carbohydrate: 21g, Dietary Fiber: 0g, Total Sugars: 12g, Protein: 0g.

94. Kava Mango Passionfruit Margarita

Enjoy this summer in the tropics with the refreshingly sweet flavor of Kava Mango Passionfruit Margarita. Get ready for a burst of tropical flavors with this vibrant fruit margarita.
Serving: Makes 4 cocktails
Preparation Time: 5 minutes
Ready Time: 5 minutes

Ingredients:
-3 ounces Kava Mix
-1/2 ounce mango puree
-1/2 ounce passion fruit puree
-1/2 cup ice (or more if needed)
-2 ounces tequila
-1 ounce triple sec
-Mango slices and fresh basil for garnish

Instructions:
1. In a blender combine Kava Mix, mango puree, passionfruit puree, tequila and triple sec.
2. Blend thoroughly, adding more ice if necessary.
3. Fill 4 glasses with a spoonful of mango slices and basil leaves.
4. Pour margarita mixture into each glass.
5. Garnish with extra mango slices and basil leaves.

Nutrition information: Per serving: Calories: 184 kcal, Carbohydrates: 11 g, Protein: 0.5 g, Fat: 0 g, Sodium: 0.3 mg.

This Kava Blackberry Sage Lemonade is a refreshing summer drink that combines the sweetness of blackberries and sage with the tang of lemon and Kava root.
Serving: Serves 2
Preparation time: 10 minutes
Ready time: 25 minutes

Ingredients:
- 1/2 cup fresh blackberries
- 1 cup ice
- 1 teaspoon Kava root powder
- 1 teaspoon minced fresh sage
- 1 cup water
- 2 tablespoons lemon juice

Instructions:
1. In a blender, blend the blackberries, ice, Kava root powder, minced sage, water and lemon juice together until combined.
2. Divide into two glasses and serve.

Nutrition information:
Calories: 27, Total Fat: 0g, Polyunsaturated Fat: 0g, Monounsaturated Fat: 0g, Sodium: 3mg, Carbohydrates: 7g, Fiber: 1g, Sugar: 4g, Protein: 0g.

Kava Cucumber Elderflower Collins is a unique and delicious twist on the classic Gin Collins. This drink is refreshing and made with only six Ingredients. It is perfect for summer gatherings or a night out.
Serving: Makes 1 drink
Preparation time: 5 minutes
Ready time: 5 minutes

Ingredients:
-2 ounces Kava spirit
-1/4 ounce lime juice
-2 ounces cucumber juice
-2 ounces elderflower liqueur
-Ice
-Soda water

Instructions:
1. Fill a martini shaker with ice.
2. Add the Kava spirit, lime juice, cucumber juice, and elderflower liqueur.
3. Shake vigorously for about 5 seconds.
4. Strain over a highball glass filled with fresh ice.
5. Top with soda water.

Nutrition information: Per serving: 110 calories; 0g fat; 0g saturated fat; 0mg cholesterol; 0mg sodium; 4g carbohydrate; 0g fiber; 0g sugar; 0g protein.

97. Kava Blueberry Pomegranate Martini

This delicious cocktail features the tropical flavors of blueberry and pomegranate combined with the creamy texture of Kava root. It is both smooth and refreshing, perfect for any occasion.
Serving: Serves 1
Preparation Time: 5 minutes
Ready Time: 5 minutes

Ingredients:
• 2 ounces kava concentrates
• 2 ounces blueberry-pomegranate juice
• 2 ounces simple syrup
• ½ ounce fresh lime juice

Instructions:
1. Place all the Ingredients in a shaker and shake until combined.
2. Strain into a martini glass.

3. Garnish with a lime wheel or wedge.

Nutrition information: Nutritional values per serving: Calories 270, Total fat 0g, Saturated fat 0g, Cholesterol 0mg, Sodium 16mg, Total carbohydrates 42g, Dietary Fiber 8g, Sugars 29g, Protein 2g.

98. Kava Lavender Lemon Spritz

Refresh your senses with this delicious Kava Lavender Lemon Spritz. It is a light and tasty infuser, made with the floral flavor of lavender and the citrusy goodness of lemon.
Servings: 2
Preparation Time: 5 minutes
Ready Time: 5 minutes

Ingredients:
- 2 ½ cups filtered water
- 2 teaspoons kava root powder
- 1 teaspoon lavender buds
- 2 tablespoons freshly-squeezed lemon juice
- 1 tablespoon honey optional

Instructions:
1. Bring the water to a light simmer in a small saucepan on medium heat.
2. Add in the kava root powder and lavender buds, stirring well and let it simmer for 5 minutes.
3. Remove from heat and pour through a strainer into two cups.
4. Stir in the lemon juice and honey, if using.

Nutrition information: Per serving, this recipe is low in calories, sodium and fat, and provides a good source of vitamin C. Calories: 15 | Total Fat: 0g | Sodium: 2mg | Total Carbohydrates: 3g | Vitamin C: 4% | Protein: 0g

99. Kava Cherry Lime Mojito

Kava Cherry Lime Mojito is a unique and creative beverage! Combine the flavors of maraschino cherries, lime, and kava kava to make a tasty and relaxing concoction. Serve with friends or family and enjoy!
Serving: 1
Preparation Time: 5 minutes
Ready Time: 5 minutes

Ingredients:
- 2 ounces of kava kava concentrate
- 2 teaspoons of maraschino cherry juice
- 2 ounces of lime juice
- 1 tablespoon of granulated sugar
- 2 tablespoons of fresh mint leaves
- Sparkling water

Instructions:
1. In a shaker or cup, combine the kava concentrate, maraschino cherry juice, lime juice, and sugar.
2. Shake or stir until the sugar has dissolved.
3. Muddle the mint leaves to release the mint flavor.
4. Add ice then pour in sparkling water.
5. Shake or stir until the Ingredients are mixed well.
6. Strain into a glass filled with ice and serve.

Nutrition information:
Calories: 167
Total Fat: 0g
Cholesterol: 0mg
Sodium: 2mg
Total Carbohydrate: 33g
Protein: 1g

100. Kava Pineapple Cilantro Margarita

This fruity and refreshing Kava Pineapple Cilantro Margarita is the perfect cocktail for your summer get-together! Served with a salted rim, this beautiful Margarita is great for entertaining and a tasty treat for your guests.

Serving: Makes 2 servings
Preparation Time: 10 Minutes
Ready Time: 10 Minutes

Ingredients:
- 2 ounces Kava
- 4 ounces pineapple juice
- 2 ounces cilantro simple syrup
- 2 ounces fresh lime juice
- 2 ounces orange liqueur
- Salted Rim

Instructions:
1. Wet rim of 2 Margarita glasses and gently press each glass into a shallow dish of coarse salt.
2. Put Kava, pineapple juice, cilantro simple syrup, lime juice and orange liqueur in a cocktail shaker. Fill with ice and shake well.
3. Divide the mixture between the two glasses, straining it with a fine mesh strainer.
4. If desired, garnish with a lime wheel or cilantro sprig.

Nutrition information: Per serving: 260 calories; 11 g fat; 32 g carbohydrates; 9 g protein; 0 mg cholesterol; 50 mg sodium.

Kava Cocktails: 100 Recipes for a Relaxing Happy Hour

In conclusion, Kava Cocktails: 100 Recipes for a Relaxing Happy Hour is an excellent cookbook that provides a variety of recipes to help you enjoy a relaxing and enjoyable happy hour. The recipes range from the traditional to the more exotic, providing something to sate every taste. The book also offers helpful tips and tricks, such as easy methods for preparing and serving kava, as well as advice on the best mixes for each drink. With its wide array of recipes and tips, this book is perfect for those looking to make the most of a relaxing and enjoyable evening. Whether you are a seasoned kava enthusiast or a beginner looking to try something new, Kava Cocktails: 100 Recipes for a Relaxing Happy Hour is an invaluable resource. Its selection of drinks and cocktails will help you create your own unique and relaxing happy hour. So what are you waiting for? Pick up a copy of this book and start enjoying a fun and relaxing evening today!

Printed in Great Britain
by Amazon